GROWING UP PERPENDICULAR
ON THE SIDE OF A HILL

CARL LEGGO

GROWING UP PERPENDICULAR
ON THE SIDE OF A HILL

CARL LEGGO

kiLLick press
an imprint of Creative Publishers
St. John's, Newfoundland
1994

Appreciation is expressed to *The Canada Council* for publication assistance.

∝ Printed on acid-free paper

Cover design: *The Perception of Mobility* by Shawn Steffler (Courtesy of the Emma Butler Gallery).

Back cover photo: Bruce McCaughey, Richmond, B.C.

Published by
KILLICK PRESS
a Creative Publishers imprint
A Division of Robinson-Blackmore Printing & Publishing
P.O. Box 8660, St. John's, Newfoundland A1B 3T7

Printed in Canada by:
ROBINSON-BLACKMORE PRINTING & PUBLISHING

Canadian Cataloguing in Publication Data

  Leggo, Carleton Derek, 1953–

    Growing up perpendicular on the side of a hill

    Poems.
    ISBN 1-895387-36-1

I. Title.

PS8573.E44G76 1994   C811'.54   C94-950114-X
PR9199.3.L44G76 1994

For my mother and father
who taught me how to live
with affection and hope
perpendicular on the side of a hill

Table of Contents

RED BUTTONS

in late autumn in the Humber Valley
afire with alder aspen larch maple
still points on a turning circle

Skipper who even as a boy dreamed
of building a boat and sailing
to Africa Australia Antarctica

skipped up Lynch's Lane washed out
in yesterday's rain to take Carrie
to the Papermaker's Ball

Carrie who danced every Saturday
with Fred Astaire in sun rain snow
at the Majestic matinee

Carrie, new graduate, now a clerk
in the mill payroll office,
going to the ball for the first time

with Skipper, apprentice electrician,
hockey player, handsome enough,
probably dances like Fred Astaire,

even has Fred Astaire's big smile,
though Carrie is not smiling,
You can't go to the dance in those pants

from waistband to crotch a line
of cherry red buttons, and Carrie's eyes
are red buttons, her nose a red button

her ears red buttons, buttons sewed
all over her face, Fred Astaire
would never wear red buttons

Skipper still smiling, Carrie, Carrie,
don't worry, I'll walk in backwards
and no one will notice, and for forty years

Carrie and Skipper have danced long
after Fred Astaire gave up and Skipper
is still navigating seas backwards

CARRIE

a few stories only
scraps from a vast store
mostly I remember you:

    making tea for Skipper

    peeling potatoes
    for french fries

    hanging laundry, red hands
    in the frosted February air

    posing for a Polaroid snap
    a new dress, eyes already
    at the New Year's Eve Dance

    walking through the city
    and the seasons, fast
    always somewhere to go

    returning with salt
    and pepper shakers shaped
    like pigs, porpoises, penguins

    a ceramic menagerie
    bagged in Woolworth's
    and Steadman's sales

    the house an ark dropped
    on the side of a hill
    you, a new Noah still
    calling the animals

    always coming, my question:
    where will you put more

a few stories only
scraps from a vast store
lost as if it never was

yet years later
I am shaking the animals
you wouldn't fill
with salt and pepper

and finding poems
waiting to be written

perhaps I am another Noah
calling the animals, too

GROWING UP PERPENDICULAR
ON THE SIDE OF A HILL

in a house hammered into a hill hanging over
the Humber Arm I grew up and watched the cargo
ships come and go without me through spring
summer autumn winter and watched Ro Carter
open the shutters on his store where
everything you ever needed could be bought and
listened for the mill steam whistle announcing
the hours and disasters always whistling

and at sixteen I left 7 Lynch's Lane Corner
Brook Newfoundland and I've been leaving for
more than two decades never staying anywhere
long enough to get to know people well enough
to have a fight an argument even and perhaps
all this time I've been running away from
Lynch's Lane where I lived a soap opera with
no commercial breaks and grew up perpendicular
on the side of a hill

with Gordie Gorman whose mother one Christmas
gave him a hunting knife with a blade like a
silver bell but Gordie Gorman refused to carve
the turkey and hunted through the house with
one clean slice down to the side cut off his
penis instead and was rushed to Montreal where
it was sewed back on though neighbours said it
never worked right again and Gordie Gorman
said only I wanted to see how sharp it was

and Francie Baker who spent a whole year in
bed just woke up on New Year's Day and said
I'm not getting up this year and day after day
just lay in bed reading the newspaper and
looking out the window and she always waved at
Cec Frazer Macky my brother and me when we
climbed the crab tree to watch her

and Tommy Stuckless the midget who we all gave
nickels to do hand-stands and somersaults and
was fierce and cranky like a crackie dog and
ran off to Toronto and became a wrestler

and Frankie Sheppard who disappeared during
his high school graduation and was found three
days later in the trees near Wild Cove mute
with the stories aswirl around his head LSD
and Old Niagara and rock music and his
girlfriend's mother finding him pinched
between her daughter's legs like a lobster

and Mikey Bishop who stopped everybody on the
road flashed open his black overcoat never
without it want to buy a watch hundreds of
watches pinned to the inside of the coat the
only thing ticking about Mikey Bishop said Cec

and Bonnie Winsor who rubbed herself with
coconut oil and lay on a red blanket in her
underwear like a movie star between sheets of
tin foil toasting in the spring sun and
sometimes smiled at Cec Frazer Macky my
brother and me hiding in the tall grass
watching her turning and cooking like a
chicken on a spit and we asked her if we could
take Polaroid snaps and she said yes but by
the time we saved up enough money for film
summer was over and Bonnie Winsor's brown body
was hidden away for another year

and Bertie Snooks who joined the army got a
haircut flew to Cornwallis and was run over by
a sergeant in a jeep without meeting the enemy
even before he completed basic training

and Sissy Fudge who was the smartest girl in
Harbourview Academy and could have been a
lawyer or doctor or engineer but had her first
baby at fifteen and almost one a year for the
next decade or two like a friggin' Coke
machine said Macky

and Janie Berkshire who built a big two-story
house with her husband Pleaman and the night
Cec Frazer Macky my brother and I carried and
dragged Pleaman all the way up Old Humber Road
and Lynch's Lane from the Caribou Tavern where
he sometimes went after prayer meetings at the
Glad Tidings Tabernacle Janie Berkshire threw
Pleaman out the new plate glass window and he
fell two stories buried in snow and Cec Frazer
Macky my brother and I hid Pleaman in Cec's
basement for the night and Janie Berkshire
painted the house magenta and raised three
daughters and served tea and walnut sandwiches
at weekly meetings with the women of Lynch's
Lane but wouldn't let Pleaman Berkshire or any
other man in the house again

and Denney Winsor whose wife ran off with an
optometrist and Denney started lifting weights
in order to beat the shit out of the
optometrist but enjoyed weightlifting so much
he shaved all the hair off his legs and chest
and came third in the Mr. Corner Brook
Bodybuilding Contest

and Sammy Sheppard who turned sixteen and
didn't want to be a boy scout or a missionary
or an honours student or a star basketball
player and took his father's lead mallet and
smashed up seven of the concrete benches at
Margaret Bowater Park until he couldn't lift
the mallet over his head anymore and spent a

few weeks in the Whitburne Detention and
Reform Center for Juveniles where he was a
model inmate

and Louella Skiffington who always wore her
fuchsia dress to the Glad Tidings Tabernacle
every Sunday and Wednesday night and for
special prayer meetings I'm devoted to the
soul-saving business she said until she came
home early one night ill and found Ronnie
Skiffington singing hymns with Amanda Parsons
the choir director and Louella stopped wearing
her fuchsia dress stopped going to the Glad Tidings
Tabernacle parked her old life like a
car wreck in the backyard and most nights
brought Greek and Portuguese second mates home
from the Caribou Tavern still saving souls the
neighbours said

but for all my running away I never escape
Lynch's Lane like the weather always mad
spring under a moon always full bonfire summer
autumn ablaze winter without end the hill
where I grew up perpendicular

LYNCH'S LANE

like black lines burned in wood
with a glass for focusing
the sun in a point
Lynch's Lane is etched in my body:

the first orange popsicle
later lime grape pineapple even
but none ever tasted as good
as the first orange popsicle
of summer with mosquitoes
sweat stinging sunburn
water and tar on the lane
to keep dust down
Skipper mowing the grass
with whistles of the scythe

autumn potatoes no bigger
than jumbo marbles boiled
in the skins sprinkled
with salt the world afire
in squashberry crumbles bakeapple jam
blueberry pies partridgeberry jelly
the wind rustling restlessly
with Cec, Frazer, Macky,
my brother, and me playing war
cricket kick the can at day's end

sucking icicles knocked from the eaves
hot cocoa drunk over the furnace grate
Old Mrs. Eaton climbing Lynch's Lane
grasping the fence like a ladder
picket after picket gasping through wool
noses pressed to frosted windows
homemade bread with Good Luck margarine
howling winter winds the house like an ark
mothers calling, Where are you going?
You can't see your noses

orange sherbet dipped in chocolate
the pink flesh of fried trout
all the neighbours in their yards
shovelling snow searching for crocuses
fallen leaves holding the sun
and cutting shapes in ice
everywhere the air lemon
smell of freshly washed cotton
the world melting splashing washing
away like saints in the River Jordan

like black lines pricked in skin
with a needle for focusing
India ink in a point
Lynch's Lane is tattooed in my body:

MY GRANDMOTHER AND KNOWLTON NASH

my grandmother's world
was framed by her bedroom window

with eyes almost blind she saw
a twilight world of shapes and shadows

the harbour and the paper cargo ships
on which her husband once sailed as cook

the world's largest pulp and paper mill
where her brother worked for a day

the Blow-Me-Down Mountains
where her father had been a guide

Meadows across the harbour and at night,
lights where a daughter's house had been

with eyes grey-sad my grandmother saw
a haphazard world, helter-skelter, no shelter

and like an air traffic controller
she tried to organize and direct her world

every night flitted back and forth
between her room and the telephone, calling,

checking on the children and grand-children,
everyone home?   everyone safe?

always flying with the northeast trade winds,
said Skipper, I wish she'd get stuck in calms

but she was forever sailing on the waves
of her fears, unending tempests

the world like the underside of a tapestry
woven by Knowlton Nash in the multicolored

threads of disaster, danger, disease, death,
destruction, depravity, debacle, damnation

when I told her from grade eight geography
Newfoundland was in the Tropic of Cancer

she was convinced we would all get cancer
and when Knowlton Nash reported the mystery

of Legionnaire's disease, my grandmother
heard engineer's disease and feared

her son and grandson, both engineers,
would get the dread unknown disease

nothing to worry about, Missus, said Skipper;
no, nothing, she replied, but I'm still

worried, and Skipper nodded, knowing
nothing cannot be fixed

and nights Skipper often drove downtown
and to the west side to confirm all was well

and nights my grandmother phoned the neighbours
of her children to confirm all was well

while death for me was almost always a fiction
on television, my grandmother knew death,

had not so much stared death in the face
as been smothered by death like heavy blankets

her father drowned on a hunting trip
a brother crushed by a hill of pulp logs

her husband lost in a truck-train collision
a daughter and three grandsons in a housefire

like my grandmother who framed her world
in a window, a resistant, uncontrollable world,

I stare through a window and try to control
my world in words like erecting cairns

to guide navigation in treacherous country
but my grandmother and Knowlton Nash

remind me constantly that the world
cannot be framed by any window

DID THE QUEEN SEE US?

in the photo
an instant of light figured:
Cec, Frazer, Macky, my brother, and I
sit on the rock in the backyard,
grins   a few teeth   mostly gaps,
holding still the Union Jacks
we'd waved waiting on West Valley Road
as Queen Elizabeth in a black Cadillac
raced Corner Brook, her first visit,
a puzzled smile, Where am I?
not seeing us at all

in the photo
an instant of life figured:
five boys who lived Lynch's Lane
as pirates knights musketeers
Green Berets Foreign Legionnaires
coureurs des bois conquistadors
Vikings Argonauts Iroquois
cowboys detectives pioneers

in the photo
a spark of light exploded:
five little boys who grew up,
wives   children   work,
still growing up
or down or sideways,
so many stories, a few only
known   in snatches only

in the photo
a spark of life exploded:
five boys now in middle age
already alive for at least
a billion seconds
a billion photos
a billion stories

stories beyond memory
stories beyond literacy
untold unread unwritten

in the photo
a rectangle of light pinned:
held in space by four triangles
isolated   story suspended
in stories,   our desire
for the camera, no fear
of lost souls, souls gained
in the photo framed

in the photo
a rectangle of life pinned:
we sat   sit   will sit on the rock
our shapes figured by light on paper,
not immortality, but shape
semblance of stable shape,
suggestive at least, like falling
in snow, fanning arms and legs,
knowing angels for a moment

FLOOD

on Lynch's Lane
we knew spring was near
when we shovelled out
fathers' cars stranded
with the first snowfall
in early November, throwing
snow and ice into the lane,
refusing to wear jackets
and mitts (so good to feel
the air biting flesh again,
we would have gone bare buff
if mothers weren't watching
from kitchen windows)
and we knew spring was here
when we built dams in snow
and ice to catch the rivulets
of melting winter,
and one spring, Cec, Macky,
Frazer, my brother, and I
built a dam we named Aswan
after a fold-out picture
in *National Geographic*,
a high white wall
like the fortress of Camelot,
and the water backed up
so deep and black even Cec
in his father's hip waders
couldn't find the deepest part
till we shouted our dynamite
explosions and the dam
burst like Noah's flood
and water rushed/gushed/shushed
down Lynch's Lane and crashed
like a tidal wave
against Maggie Mercer's house
and washed the creaking
house off its foundation

and swept Maggie Mercer
and her house and all
the little and big Mercers
out into the harbour
and around Halfway Point
into the Strait of St. Lawrence
and the Atlantic Ocean,
and every Christmas I receive
a card from Maggie Mercer
in Tahiti or Australia
in Fiji or Madagascar

HAIRCUT

the neighbours said
Harvey Balsam was mad
as a crackie
with Limey LeDrew
because Limey LeDrew
grew up in England,
spoke with an English accent,
and made more money
than he could spend
by cutting up sick people,
while Harvey Balsam
grew up in Crow Gulch,
pronounced "oar" like "whore"
and "hate" like "ate"
and, even doing well
in his barber shop
with a third chair recently
added, would never make
enough for a huge house over-
looking the Bay of Islands,
and just before Christmas
Limey LeDrew dropped
into Harvey's for a shave,
but failed to hear
filling the air
music about love,
God, and Santa Claus,
too busy explaining
to Harvey and the neighbours
how barbers and surgeons
were once the same,
haircutting and bloodletting,
both available at the shop
with the candystripe pole,
and next day Derek LeDrew,
only eleven, sat in Harvey's
chair and declared

in his private school accent
learned at King's College,
Nova Scotia that he needed
a precise and careful haircut
because his family was spending
Christmas vac in Jamaica
when Harvey Balsam heard
a choir of angels, spun
the chair away from the mirror,
shaved Derek LeDrew bald
like a pale pink jaw breaker,
and crowed to the neighbours,
Barbers don't have
a hypocritic oath

ANTONIO

Antonio's hair was Samson long
and in plaits knotted
to a rope Antonio
(WORLD'S MIGHTIEST MAN)
could pull two, even three,
buses, could lift a car,
could wrestle a dozen little men

and walking Dove's Road
I was Antonio pulling
a parade of yellow buses
when I saw the wide, black Plymouth,
sagging on the driver's side,
saw the door open,
saw Antonio climb up,
wide and dark like the Plymouth,
squeeze into Hutchings' Store

and I waited
      waited
Antonio in the door
with a bag of apples
and I knew he'd eat the apples
in single bites,
eat them like cherries
and not even spit out the seeds,
and his mouth opened, big
yellow teeth nibbled
like a grandmother sipping
tea-soaked toast through her gums

and that night at Humber Gardens
Antonio pulled buses
and stomped in a ring littered
with bodies and lifted
the front of a Volkswagen
but all I saw was Antonio nibbling
and I didn't clap and for weeks
I wouldn't eat apples

JIMMY THE JACKRABBIT

sometimes on Sundays
I went with Frazer
to the Glad Tidings Tabernacle
   where sins were seized
      shackled scoured stamped
   where souls were saved
      sated salted sealed
according to Jimmy the Jackrabbit
who wound himself up with words
   about the wide way
   and the narrow way
words forged out of fired faith
as he jabbed jumped jogged
crisscrossing the platform
like a stocky Mick Jagger
taunting the devil to wrestle him
for souls wallowing in sin
and one night Jimmy the Jackrabbit
   filled with the spirit
      leap-frogged the pulpit
   danced off the platform
      over the backs of pews
   sprayed spit spite sparks
      while the brothers and sisters
   split like the Red Sea
      charged out of the church
but obviously didn't find
the Promised Land of milk and honey
because soon he rushed back,
Can hell be any worse than
the world outside these walls?,
   his words swirling about
   like a squall trapped
   in crosscurrents of wind

and with a convert's conviction
I knew I would never again
jig with Jimmy the Jackrabbit
in the Glad Tidings Tabernacle

WHERE DO BABIES COME FROM?

the summer the sky was blue
only, early morning, noon,
twilight, even midnight blue,
and the air was dust
gray, still, like flannel
blankets on a clothesline,
and everyone hid in basements
or sat on verandas sucking
lime, raspberry, grape, pineapple
popsicles, I hunted lions
and ferocious head-shrinkers
hiding in the tall grass
in Sadie Gillam's backyard,
and found a baby in a shoebox,
a gray wrinkled baby like a kitten,
and took it to my mother
who cried for Skipper
playing darts in the basement,
and Skipper took the box away
and nobody would tell me
where the baby came from
where the baby went
and all summer I hunted lions
and head-shrinkers
in Sadie Gillam's yard
but I never again
found a baby

DAISY GRIFFIN

crawling through the tall grass
in Sammy Baker's back yard
hunting for grasshoppers
I saw Jimmy Griffin's mother
framed in her picture window,
the only time I ever saw
her, a phantom, a character
in a story, not that I knew much
about Jimmy Griffin, the only
Catholic on Lynch's Lane

Cec, Frazer, Macky, my brother,
and I, all Protestants
whose only protest was going
to church, had little to do
with Jimmy Griffin who wore
a blue blazer and was an altar boy,
but I saw Daisy Griffin
in the window, her eyes fixed
on the harbour or the sky or beyond,
and the neighbours hinted Daisy was

   : a lush
   : married to God
   : always pregnant
   : too good for anybody
   : a looney

but I saw Daisy Griffin,
a pale face framed
in black hair, framed
in the window, like a child
on a stormy day, both fascinated
and fearful with the world outside,
and I wanted Daisy Griffin
to crawl through the tall grass
in Sammy Baker's back yard
hunting for grasshoppers, too

BATTLE

driven by Saturday western and war matinees
Cec, Frazer, Macky, my brother, and I
fought renegades, enemies, desperadoes,
built forts and camps and bomb shelters
in snow and scrap lumber and blankets,
and saved the world for God and democracy
and civilization in bloody vicious battles
(truces only for meals)
wielding wooden and Woolworth's guns
and sawed up broom handles for grenades
and snowballs melted to lethal iciness
and screams to curdle grandmother's blood,
but the real battle took place
on a June afternoon outside Penney's store
when Bobby Buckle, dark and mean
like a wolverine, threatened to rip
my nose and ears off if I didn't give him
my Mountain Dew and Cherry Blossom bar,
and I knew the hand grenades in my pockets
and the karate I'd practised on Cec
and even the cap pistol in my belt
weren't much good against Bobby Buckle
and I was swallowing a hard knob of fear
and the harder need to surrender
when Macky said, Shit off, Buckle,
and Bobby Buckle's eyes went from black
like licorice to black like onyx
filled with fire and his hands closed
into dense metal balls, silver and flaring,
and Macky, a pillar of rock, stared
at Bobby Buckle who glared and cursed,
but Macky didn't even blink his eyes,
and Bobby Buckle swung around like a cyclone,
missed Macky and continued spinning
all the way down Harbourview Road,
and I let Macky have the cherry
in my Cherry Blossom bar

MACKY'S MYOPIA

the hot August afternoon
the warship Assiniboine
lined from a gray iceberg
loomed in the Humber Arm
with enough guns and bombs
to explode all Corner Brook
Macky got his glasses

our mothers muttered,
Don't dare go near the CN wharf,
and Cec, Frazer, my brother, and I
scared of mothers, really spies
sat all afternoon on the cliff
over the harbour and watched
sailors in snow white suits

while Macky, a red-haired rod
of unbent steel, was drawn
by the Assiniboine till he leaned
over the wharf and saw
his new glasses turn
circles in the air into the harbour
where a cod still wears them

Cec, Frazer, my brother, and I
didn't expect to see Macky
again, but a few days later
he showed up in our shack
of spruce boughs in the woods,
The other day when I wore glasses
you guys looked a lot uglier

CHIPS

the morning my brother danced
out of the house, his first summer job,
    Got you a job, son, at George's Diner,
    work hard, job could last all summer,
    might even chop potatoes for chips,
Carrie, Nan, my sister, and I
all stood in the backdoor and waved
as Skipper and my brother eased
down Lynch's Lane under an opal sky,
Skipper's broad smile gleaming
like the grill on his Chevy II,
and at day's end we all stood
in the backdoor again to greet
George's new employee, the apprentice chef,
we called him, when the Chevy II crawled
up Lynch's Lane with Skipper's head
jutted out the side window,
his face a pickled beet, barking,
    Shit, up to his knees in shit,
echoes off the Blow-Me-Down Mountains,
my brother, his face shiny yellow-white
like a thin slice of potato, muttered,
    I shovelled out George's septic tank,
and long after midnight Skipper still sat
in the backyard, sipping Old Sam and Coke
while my brother soaked in Skin-So-Soft
for six or seven baths, sometimes shouting,
    Shovelling shit was fun

NELLIE EVANS

on the last day
of each month
Mr. Banfield adorned
in a brand new blue suit
and matching overcoats
for the seasons
lumbered up Lynch's Lane
to read the meters

end of July Mr. Banfield
poked his head
in Nellie Evans' door
Nellie and her daughters
making bread each wearing
a pair of panties
faded opal pink blue
on her head

who needed hair nets
though Nellie said
probably the panties
made Mr. Banfield
say what he said,
If you girls treated
me better, your bill
wouldn't be so high

Nellie and her daughters
eyed blue Mr. Banfield
dumped a can of flour
on him chased him down
Lynch's Lane hurtling
lumps of dough
a winter storm in July
Nellie's bill went up up

THE DIVER

In the gray-blue sky my brother hung,
long and lean, his body a line
lined with taut muscles, and Macky's
mouth was a gaping hole in a scream
or laugh because my brother was making
the death-defying dive never dared
from the concrete abutment at the end
of the dam where the water was no more
than a foot deep though it got deeper,
out and out (if only you could fly
and my brother loved to fly).

> Earlier in the summer
> my brother climbed the arch
> of heavy timbers that hold
> the dam in place, and golden
> in the falling sun, high
> above our heads, he flew
> through the air and sliced
> the water, and was gone,
> and Frazer moaned, He's dead,
> but my brother emerged
> slowly like a submarine,
> and though he was silent
> I saw the quick smile.

In the still air my brother hung,
blonde and brown and blue, his head
tucked between his arms, hands clenched,
body a missile, toes pointed back
like jet engines, and Cec shouted, He's
doin' it, holy smoke, and my brother
needed to dive far out like shooting
off a rocket launch pad, out and out,
and since he knew he couldn't move fast
enough to reach orbit, knew he would come
down, he had to skip over the water

like a racing boat or run aground
on the rocky bottom.

Earlier in the summer
my brother chased his shadow
across the grass and leaped
off the rock, flying, shooting
just under the surface
like a torpedo, and Macky
grinned, He dives so shallow,
he hardly breaks the water,
but my brother just looked
at us with no smile
though I saw the purple sky
reflected in his eyes.

The gray-blue sky and still air broke
and my brother dropped, but he
didn't skip once, twice, three
times in quick smooth skips, and plunged
into the black water, and my eyes closed
but wouldn't stay closed, and my brother
stood in the water up to his knees.

I can't recall the dive
as a series of movements;
I remember only the still
moment when my brother hung
in the gray-blue sky
and that other moment
when he stood in the water
stained with his blood,
raw and bloody
like a skinned rabbit,
his eyes darting, searching,
as if he'd awaken
in a brightly lit room
he didn't know.

O

I was on a toboggan, standing up,
like a California surfer, like Frankie Avalon
flying straight out down Lynch's Lane
all the way from Old Man Downey's house
riding the blue-white snow, over the first
boy-built bump, rope tied tightly
around my mitt like a bronco buster's grip,
and Cec shouting words I thought were curses
because he'd never made it from the top
      and I was going to,
the hill and snow and toboggan and me
all one like a postcard from Austria,
over the last bump, bracing for the sharp bend
where Lynch's Lane twists into Bannister's Road
shooting through the air with a grin
frozen on my face, the letters E-S-S-O
growing bigger and bigger until I dived into the
                        O
a perfect bull's-eye, and woke up the next day
singing Old MacDonald had a farm
                  EIEIO
and Cec said he was glad I wasn't dead,
but I knew darn sure he was just glad
I was stopped by the truck
and not still surfing all the way
through the O and around the world.

A COFFIN AND A CHEVY

My father bought the '58 Chevy,
maroon and new, drove my brother and me
out of the city along the Trans Canada Highway
to cut a Christmas tree, parked on the shoulder,
left my brother and me, sank into the snow
like quicksand, my brother, only four, laughing,
and I was laughing at my brother laughing
as my father waved a hand, his mouth a tight line,
just before he was swallowed by snow and dark trees
and my brother jumped up and down in the back seat
while I pretended to drive away for help
but went nowhere, and my father didn't come back,
my brother full of fear, no longer laughing,
and the air was thick with chewy toffee,
my father gone, my brother going crazy,
so I grabbed the ice scraper and jabbed holes
in the maroon velvet over me like the inside
of a coffin, no escape, and my father returned,
creature from the snow lagoon, bearing a tree,
a wide grin where the line had been,
and the car was a car, not a coffin,
my father was alive, my brother was laughing,
and my father looked at the neat triangular flags
hanging from the ceiling of his new Chevy,
said nothing, drove back to the city
in a Chevy once more a coffin.

THE BED

at Coleman's Furniture World
my mother bought the bed
French provincial queen
gleaming enamel white
etched in lines of gold

a bed too grand for sleeping in
and when Mother and Skipper left
on Saturday night for Merle's
I watched my grandmother nap with Bob Barker
and sneaked a step-ladder into the bedroom

my brother and I, the Leggoni brothers
aerial artists extraordinaire
jumped   flew   tumbled   dived
from the ladder in the air to the bed
a trampoline for bouncing to the moon

I was practising my brother's trademark
double pike somersault with a twist
when the trampoline no longer bounced
and my heart broke with long hard cracks
my grandmother crying, Oh my, oh my

the next morning my father called
my brother and me into his room
looked at us hard and harder,
Boys, you've hurt your mother, hurt
her bad; what can you do about it?

what could we do? I didn't know
and still don't   Skipper strapped
the bed together with black electrical tape
and it stayed that way for at least
a decade, at least until I left home

A.R.S.E.

one Saturday just weeks before Christmas
on the trail between Quinton and Bannister's
Cec, Frazer, Macky, my brother, and I
slid on floor canvas Cec's father
always watching Mr. Fix-it had ripped up
in another home improvement project

all day we tumbled toppled tripped
till late afternoon in a shower of snow light
with mothers in kitchen doors calling supper
Old Man Giles with the coal cart
coaxed the horse he named A.R.S.E.
down the trail where they slipped

on canvas we had left in the snow
I didn't do it you did we all said
but each of us knew the canvas was ours
and A.R.S.E. glided all the way
an ice sculpture on a magic carpet
and stumbled only at the bottom

into a bank of snow all day no one
had slid the whole trail standing up
and we ran down to congratulate A.R.S.E.
but Old Man Giles was sitting in the snow
his eyes gold fire in the street light
his horse's head in his lap

black eyes and black blood seeping
the horse's heart pierced
with a splinter of maple cracked stave
I said we'll pull the cart for you
Old Man Giles said I can't replace
A.R.S.E. with a bunch of asses

THE MECCANO SET

I recall only one Christmas Eve on Lynch's Lane
with the distinct edges of a photograph
the others all mixed together like jujubes
in a glass jar   only one Christmas Eve
when I prayed for a Meccano set for building
skyscrapers and bridges and towers in the air
the Meccano I didn't get while Grant Bower did

the fathers dropped in for a drink, a small one,
Skipper, and sang with Bing Crosby singing
in the snow, the snowfalling, always falling,
on Lynch's Lane while my grandmother danced
from window to window watching for Santa Claus
with reports about the weather and neighbours
and this Christmas Eve we all danced with her

the air afire   red light   broken
curses   Grant's father in his underwear
staggered in the lane   retched pictures
in the snow   clung to the fence
police pulled him   dragged him
like a toboggan   Grant and his mother
watched   watched him taken away

I recall that Christmas Eve because Grant
got the Meccano set I wanted and didn't get
and all winter he wouldn't let me play with it
and in June Grant and his mother moved away
and I bought his Meccano set for three dollars
still wrapped in plastic and built sturdy towers
of steel that couldn't be knocked down

A WISE MAN BEARING GIFTS

Christmas Eve
      Uncle Sam
(the seventh son of a seventh son
claimed he was blessed
with magical power
to spirit away warts
though I'd never seen him do it)

drunk (often, too often
drunk, my mother said)

stood in the doorway
his face round and red
like a Macintosh apple

bore a small box
with a big mauve bow

said, For Skipper
(a bottle of Avon
aftershave shaped
like a horse's head)

said, Skipper, I brought you
the 'arse's 'ead,
you're a good friend
(spit in a stutter)
but I kept
the 'arse's arse for myself

Christmas Eve
      Uncle Sam
(the seventh son of a seventh son)
spirited away a lot of warts

ICEBERG

like prairie dogs
Cec, Frazer, Macky,
my brother and I
burrowed tunnels
in the mountains of snow
plowed pushed packed
along Lynch's Lane
by fire-yellow tractors,
twisted tunnels,
long, often dark,
always narrow,
where we broke out
of Alcatraz and East Berlin,
but I remember mostly
the foiled escapes:
stuck upside down
in a tight vertical tunnel,
my parka too bulky
to negotiate the right angle
into a horizontal tunnel,
my tears and screams
melting the snow
into a glacial prison,
I was trapped
in an iceberg,
forever preserved
like the mammoths in Siberia
with undigested plants
still intact in their stomachs,
when the boys pulled me
up by the feet
into the equatorial noon sun
of their laughter
where I longed
for my iceberg prison

MORSE CODE

for years
every Wednesday night
every Friday night
Zeke Ezekiel
played darts
in the Caribou Tavern
got drunk
had the shit
beat out of him
was left outside
the tavern door
for his mother
on her way home
from bingo
until Timmy O'Reilly
sent Zeke spinning
into Western Memorial
where Zeke woke
the next day
every day
paralyzed
his eyes alone
flicking flitting
his mother teaching
him Morse code
flashing his eyes
slow quick winks
but none of us
could tell
if Zeke's eyes
spelled
   kiss me
   kill me
so we kissed Zeke
like we adored him
like he was the pope
and avoided his eyes

PENCILS

every day on his way home from work
in the town office as a town planner
(though Jed's father always complained
he could see no evidence of planning
in the town), Cyril Kelloway, a bachelor
with a face like January snow and arms
like alder branches, visited Cashin's Store
for no better reason, the neighbours said,
than to get a look, just a look, at Sadie Cashin
who'd been Miss Labour Day two or three
decades ago (Jed said she should be called
Mrs. Labour Lay after eleven children, all boys
except for Maisie Lee), and every day
Cyril bought a pencil: Writing a big book,
going to be published in Toronto, he said,
(Skipper alone agreed Cyril was smart
enough to write a book), and one Sunday afternoon
while picking wild strawberries along the railway
track, Cec, Frazer, Macky, my brother and I
found Cyril lying across the tracks, dead
with a broken heart, according to the neighbours,
a heart attack, according to the doctor,
and Skipper was asked by Cyril's brother
who built skyscrapers in Boston to clear out
Cyril's apartment, sell everything, and bury Cyril,
and Skipper found no manuscript, only a whole trunk
of unsharpened pencils

THE CONCRETE BOAT

In the long winter
my father built a concrete boat
shaped in chicken wire and cement
(asked why he didn't just build
a wooden boat, he mumbled,
Old Joe Hall, at least
seventy-five years close
to the grave, is building
a wooden boat, anybody can build
a wooden boat), built his concrete boat
and sailed into the August morning
sun like a dollop of margarine
laughing farewells to mother and promises
of gifts from Greece and Mauritius
and sailed across the Humber Arm
into the sun and was gone
and I knew he'd never come back
but the next day the kitchen door
opened and my father was back,
his face twisted in a shy grin:
The concrete boat sailed like a dead cod;
a big wave spit me up on shore
outside the harbour near Dunphy's plant;
I should've built with wood.

I'M ALONE

two ways to build a boat, says Uncle Jim,
pounding each nail with three swings
so exact and rhythmic you'd think
he was a rechargeable Black and Decker hammer;
you can start from scratch and dream the plans
in the air and on paper or you can begin
with an old boat and replace each plank and rib,
piece by piece, until the old boat is firewood
and the new boat is the old boat's image;
the second way is slower, but I like a boat
with family connections; so Uncle Jim built
a plastic shack over the beached skiff,
years earlier named the *I'm Alone*
after a rum-running schooner that plied
the eastern seaboard, and searched the autumn
woods for timbers and laid the new keel
in November and the ribs in December
with Bud and Skipper and Fox dropping by
to offer advice and clint nails,
but the boat-building stopped in January
when Uncle Jim drove Fox up to Corner Brook
to the hospital, Fox smiling through his pain
that he was okay, but he wasn't okay
with most of his stomach cancer-eaten,
and all through the winter Uncle Jim
couldn't work on the *I'm Alone*
while Fox died daily and died finally in May,
and in the summer that spring
didn't make it to the top of the hills
Uncle Jim began building the *I'm Alone* again,
wishing a person could be replaced,
plank by plank, rib by rib, as easily as a boat

RAGS

Looking through the kitchen window
from the middle of the floor
so Lavinia Mullins can't see us looking:
in her yard a line of silk, satin,
chiffon flags like robin's eggs
and Scotch mints and pup's bellies
from Frederick's in Hollywood
and the Co-op downtown, enough
silk, satin, chiffon for a Persian
king's harem (like Hugh Hefner
Lavinia Mullins wears only pajamas)

and in mid-morning Lavinia afire in magenta,
four or five or six Mullins children
half-consumed in the flames of her gown,
everyone laughing, Carrie, my line's filled,
again, may I use yours? and mother's line
sagging with Mullin's sun-bleached, gray,
washed-out flannel, denim, worsted,
like wash day in an army boot camp

and mother complaining to Skipper,
Lavinia always hangs the rags on my line;
what are the neighbours thinking?
and Skipper, snoring softly under his newspaper,
I don't care where she hangs her drawers,
while I dreamed of sparing mother,
crawling across the lane in darkness,
G.I. Joe on a suicide sabotage mission,
and Skipper, still snoring, We can live
with rags on our line; perhaps she can't,

and mother said nothing, sometimes counted
the shades of pink on Lavinia's line,
while years passed and our neighbours perhaps
noted Mullins' gray rags like cobwebs
until one August morning Lavinia lit our line

with the colours of fire, locked her gate,
gave a carload of Mullins children to aunts,
and entered a sanatorium where she wore
only white flannel, and mother wrapped
Lavinia Mullins' nighties with the French names
in tissue paper and kept them in a box
under her bed, for Lavinia, but Lavinia
didn't come back.

SNAPSHOTS

on August 6 my father spoke
    two words only   hello
    dropped the phone
a still silent world exploded
charged through the door
    leaped the steps
       raced the field
          jumped the fence
barged into Mrs. Pollard's house
    was gone
I chased him and sat on a rock
in the August morning air
the world silent still once more
    waited
    a long time
the blue sky exploded
fell around my feet
the siren like shards of glass
the ambulance men, the stretcher
my father, Mrs. Pollard
her face white like a beachstone
red with lipstick or blood
my father looked at me
his mouth opened and closed
the word   dead   hung
in the air all day
    for many days

NECKTIES

one year Jimmy Hackett bought his father
neckties for birthday and anniversary,
Easter and Christmas, in shades of gray
like bank managers wear and on New Year's Eve
his father sat at the kitchen table staring
into a bottle with no Captain Morgan
and no ship with furled sails waiting
for winds to sail the seven seas
and Jimmy Hackett helped his father
up the stairs to bed where he lay as if dead
even through neighbours' gun salutes
and Guy Lombardo playing Auld Lang Syne
and shouts from the daughter in Toronto
who never forgot to phone the best new year yet
and Jimmy Hackett lashed his father
to the bed with neckties and sprinkled him
with kerosene and lit a bonfire
and police and paramedics and psychologists
all asked why, and Jimmy Hackett only replied,
He wasn't going to wear the neckties anyway

BUZZ

My father's
friend Buzz
wanted to give
up working
in the mill
and become
a dentist,
wanted it so
bad he couldn't
think about anything
else until he was
sure everybody
was plotting
against him
scheming to make
sure he could
never be
a rich dentist
and he smothered
his wife under
a pillow till
she wasn't breathing
and got sent
to the Waterford
where he's been
sitting
in a corner
reading
for the last
twelve years
and now
he's getting out
and my father
hopes
he doesn't
come to visit.

GOING DOWN THE ROAD

in the summer of polio and t.b.
Billy Mercer dug a big hole
in his slant backyard to park
his new car, decided finally
everyone else had one
he wanted one too, dug the hole,
bought a buttercup yellow car,
sat in the car in the hole
day after day, season after season
pretending to go somewhere
but went nowhere, told Skipper,
I don't have anywhere to go
and the license plate stayed the same
while more than a decade passed
with Billy Mercer's car rooted
in the backyard, buttercup yellow
among the lupines daisies hollyhocks
until under a full spring moon
the Noble boys got drunk, yanked
the car out of Billy Mercer's backyard
rolled it down Harbourview Road
(Billy Mercer on his verandah shouting,
That's no way to drive a car)
past Tobins Ezekiels Fudges Pikes
across Dove's Road and Old Humber Road
through a plate glass window
and a pyramid of Christie Crackers
into Ro Carter's General Store
and next day customers who came
for salt beef and popsicles
walked around/through/over the car
(Billy Mercer sitting behind the wheel
to demonstrate how it ought to be driven)
and Ro Carter said only,
I'm expanding the business,
Carter's Cars, want to buy a car?

WILD COVE

at Wild Cove our mothers cooked jig's dinner,
salt beef, potatoes, turnip greens, carrots,
peas pudding, on Coleman stoves and our fathers
took off their shirts and socks, their flesh
after a winter lifetime in the paper mill
like freshly kneaded bread dough, and baked
in the sun and sand, while we hid in the trees
waiting for girls to change into bathing suits
and spelled dirty limericks in the red clay
at the end of the cove where Old Man Piercey
lived in a shack and once threw peppermint
knobs at us and floated across the cove
on inner tubes, the water blacker and blacker
the deeper out we went and mothers always
complaining we went out too far, far too far,
and on an August afternoon when the world was
baked blue-green enamel, a small car,
aquamarine like a tropical sea, rolled slowly
down the gravel hill to the beach, didn't stop,
rolled toward the water, into the water,
didn't sink, floated, started to churn waves
and cruise across the cove on a yellow wave
road of sunlight and was gone and I knew God
drove a car like that, even though the mothers
asked, Isn't a car a car and a boat a boat?
and years later I still wish I had hooked
my inner tube to the car and drove/sailed
all the world's continents and seas

ANTHONY'S NOSE

when Anthony moved to Lynch's Lane
Cec, Frazer, Macky, my brother, and I knew

we would never be Cec, Frazer, Macky,
Anthony, my brother, and I; knew

in rain he wore a yellow plastic coat
that covered his knees and a yellow cap
as if carved out of a block of margarine

in snow he wore navy nylon pants
like babies and girls always wore
and when he walked he swished/swashed

he carried his homework and lunch
in a leather briefcase like fathers
on T.V. carried to their offices

his mother bought his clothes
in the Eaton's catalogue
and he tried to look like the Beatles

but crazy as he was, we still liked him
and his basement filled with toys
he didn't even care if we broke

in the cool September twilight he joined us
in the field behind Mugs O'Reilly's house
plotting a raid on Cy Gill's apple tree

his nose was red pepper skinned raw
like a baboon's bottom, but he was silent,
just handed us a scrap of paper

DO YOU WANT SPOTLESS SKIN?
REMOVE ZITS WITH OUR
ZIT ZAPPER

a woman, the kind seen only in magazines,
a funnel-shaped device over her nose
with a cord plugged into a wall

Anthony stared into the heather-blue sky
like he wasn't sure what kept it up:
didn't work; almost sucked my nose off

that night we stole Cy Gillam's apples
and Anthony stopped wearing the rain coat
and cap and snow pants and briefcase

the next summer he moved off Lynch's Lane
but Cec, Frazer, Macky, my brother, and I

knew if he had stayed we would have been
Cec, Frazer, Macky, Anthony, my brother, and I

I RESCUE DEL CASHIN

on our hill Del Cashin was a princess
with auburn hair that fell past her bum

sometimes she leaned on her verandah rail
shook her hair over her shoulders and sang

perhaps when my hair reaches far enough
you boys will climb up and rescue me

and Cec, Frazer, Macky, my brother, and I
were knights afire with desire for Del

though we had no idea why she needed rescuing
what wily wizards and witches were waiting

knew only that we were chosen to save Del
spent whole days swinging in the alders

below her house waiting for the call always
ready with swords of alder and loops of rope

until an August afternoon Del pushed pulled
her Westinghouse wringer washer to the verandah

and in the dusty blue air hung her underwear
a horizontal strip tease in reverse

whispered moans in the alders stopped only
with Del's scream each of us falling running

I climbed the trellis to the verandah first
found Del yelling thrashing blindly

almost swallowed by the wringer washer
her hair caught in the rollers like a dish towel

and with the knife Baden Powell promised
would save my life if I was lost in the jungle

I cut off Del's hair and Del said thanks
but you might have unplugged the machine

Del's knights said nothing stared at Del
almost bald her face pinched pink wrinkled

the next day Clyde's Furniture delivered
an automatic washer Del stored in the basement

Del's rescuers stopped swinging in alders
I guess Del's hair grew back I can't remember

MOLASSES

on a silver winter night
my brother threatened to pour molasses
on my homework (What kind of house
did Bunga the Pygmy live in?)
his grinning threat, my whining complaint
filling the kitchen air with purple
while my father in the living room
worked a crossword puzzle
(a five-letter word for regret,
unsolvable with sons, a four-letter word)
until he charged into the kitchen
and my brother shot out the door
speeding through the snow in his socks
with my father on the trail of hot footprints
like Bunga's father hunting a wild hog
up Lynch's Lane, over Mamie Jenkins'
picket fence through wind-swept drifts
riddled with tunnels and traps
after a weekend of boys' busy burrowing
and I was still listing Bunga's favorite foods
when my brother's head poked around the door
blowing poison darts from cinnamon eyes
but I only grinned, and my father tracked
wet footprints across the kitchen floor
into my brother's room while I waited
in the deep, still house, then leaving Bunga
digging yams, I sneaked toward my brother's door,
I'm sorry I chased you, my father's voice,
light blue, and the next day I couldn't
read my Bunga homework because the pages
were dark and soggy with molasses

FIRE

in the Sahara-dry summer,
heat like a dusty musty rug,
everyone on Lynch's Lane wheezing
asthmatically in the peasoup
mustard peanut butter air,
houses exploded

God's judgment, Armageddon
on the doorstep, announced Uncle Esau;
spontaneous combustion, heat build-up,
boasted Dale, grade ten chemist;
arson, bad luck, evil spirits,
arsin' around, revenge, smoking in bed,
mumbled/whispered/wheezed others:
and only I knew though I couldn't tell

after Mugs O'Reilly's big boarding house
burned for twelve hours, the firemen left
a black rubble and I wished
I'd never hidden in the tall elm
outside Bonnie Lee's window
hoping to see her undress

Buck Cunningham's house hooked
into the side of a rock burned
and Buck like a baby crying
and running around in his underwear
telling the firemen what to do,
and I wished I'd never hidden
in the tall grass and discussed
with the boys what it would be like
to do it with Bonnie Lee and I
wasn't even sure what doing it was

and Maisie Shepherd's house burned
and I wished I'd never stared at ladies'
underwear on clotheslines, looked
at *True Detective* and *Stag* in Tom's store
when Tom wasn't looking, stood under the
iron stairway to look up Miss Robson's
dress, gave Eddy Mosher my recess money
to draw pictures of naked women, once
watched Jed and Pikey play strip poker
with Jan and Holly in the shack of spruce
boughs and cardboard deep in the woods

and I was Shadrach, Meshach, and Abednego
walking through fire a pyromaniac
in an asbestos suit firing the world

LOVE STORIES

on weekends Lenny Hynes lived on Lynch's Lane,
every weekend, with Nellie Nippard and four
little Nippards whose father had gone to
Labrador to work on the Churchill Falls hydro
project and fallen down a turbine shaft, every
Friday about five minutes after the five o'clock
whistle Lenny Hynes climbed Lynch's Lane with an
empty lunch basket, and the little Nippards
played in the yard until bedtime, summer and
winter, and every Monday morning Lenny Hynes
went back to the mill, worked all day, and just
after the five o'clock whistle went home to the
west side of Corner Brook where he spent Monday
night to Friday morning with his wife and three
daughters

Fran Fudge had five children with five fathers
none of whom spent more than five years with her
at five Lynch's Lane

Vern and Vera Vokey were married almost two
decades when they took in Claude Quigley as a
boarder, and for another two decades they all
lived together, and it was commonly known that
Vera and Claude were lovers though nobody ever
asked, just gossiped, and some of us pondered
the sleeping arrangements, figured Vera and
Claude were having a good time while Vern
watched "Bonanza," did they take turns? all
three together?, and Priscilla Peddle kept
saying, I don't know what they see in her, she's
just skin and bones, until one late June evening
Vera watched Claude drown off the log boom in
Deer Lake, and Vera scared half to death had a
stroke, and died months later after lying in bed
moaning, Claude, Claude, nothing more, leaving
Vern alone, and everyone noted how good he
looked, happy even

Hope Baldwin and Gil Budgell went together for
fifty years, went to weddings and funerals,
visited daily, picked berries, discussed the
weather, and as far as anyone knows never spent
a night together in fifty years, went nowhere
without Hope's brother Vince

Mrs. Peddle walked up Old Humber Road on her way
home from the Caribou Tavern with Clyde Hackett
who sold furniture on Broadway, Clyde had sold
her a bed and was going to test it,
satisfaction guaranteed was his motto, two
o'clock in the morning, met Skipper and Carrie
walking down Old Humber Road on their way home
from Wellon's, Clyde just smiled, almost always
smiled anyway, Mrs. Peddle said, I'm planning to
buy a washer, and Skipper said, One of the new
automatic washers?, and Mrs. Peddle said, It's
time I got one with six kids, and Skipper said,
Yes, it is, the next morning Skipper was mowing
the grass, long sweeps with the scythe,
whistling in the grass, and Mrs. Peddle stood at
the fence and called, The washer is coming today
or tomorrow, and Skipper said, Good, it'll be a
big help

Stephanie and her lover were found in a Mustang
alongside the Humber River twelve hours after
Stephanie's mother reported her missing, knotted
together in the backseat of the Mustang still
purring poison through rust holes in the floor,
and it wasn't easy to pry them apart and bury
them in separate plots, Love and that
foolishness, said some of the neighbours

when Cassandra Noseworthy fell in love with Noel
Payne everyone on Lynch's Lane watched Lucinda
Payne to see what she would do, but she did
nothing, pretended that Cassandra and Noel
weren't thick as flies around a dead connor,

pretended that Cassandra didn't visit Noel while
she rang doorbells and waved unwanted Avon,
pretended that Noel was playing darts at the
Caribou Tavern even though he was never there
when she looked in on her way home from bingo,
pretended that Noel was still in love with her
as he had been when they were eighteen and he
got her pregnant in a snowbank behind Carter's
store, but she stopped pretending when Noel told
her he was going fishing with his buddies for a few
days and Lucinda ran into his buddies who didn't
know where he was, and she drove all over
the Bay of Islands, down the north shore to
Cox's Cove and the south shore to Lark Harbour,
as far as Deer Lake going east and finally after
two days of driving she found Noel, going west,
at Dhoon Lodge near Stephenville Crossing, and
shot Cassandra with a duck-hunting shotgun while
she crouched behind the bathroom door, but
Lucinda wouldn't shoot Noel with the other
barrel because she hoped he might still come
back to her, and Lucinda died about fifteen
years later in Kingston Penitentiary, still
waiting for Noel who went every week to visit
Cassandra's grave

TRUE ROMANCE

on Lynch's Lane I had many heroes
daily watched John Wayne Matt
Dillon the Lone Ranger Tonto Roy
Rogers Trigger Huckleberry Hound
the Cartwrights Fred MacMurray
Hogan's Heroes Maxwell Smart Tarzan
Walt Disney Rin Tin Tin Lucy Ed
Sullivan Jed Clampett Quickdraw
McGraw Number 99 Batman Gordon
Pinsent the Cleavers Bugs Bunny
right a wrong world

and I needed heroes with the mad
Mercers out the living room kitchen
bedroom windows Mercers watching
everywhere round us like sharks
after old man Mercer divided
his strip from Harbour to Heights
divided it in parcels big parcels
for the sons little parcels
for the daughters and went away
to shoot a moose and never came back

leaving Billy Mercer sitting
in the dark watching black and white
television through sunglasses
afraid of ultraviolet rays

and Lil Mercer who hid in her house
all winter but danced naked
in her front yard under the full May moon
and spent summer on the fifth floor
of the Western Memorial Regional Hospital

and Sam Mercer on his verandah
drinking rum watching the world go by
wondering where the world was going
since he'd never gone further
than he could see from his verandah

and Sal Mercer who talked without end
and never said a word I can remember
using words to fend off the darkness
the terrible darkness around her

and Dougie Mercer who survived polio
tuberculosis diabetic comas cancer
for more than eight decades with words
like talismans you don't have to worry
about me I won't be here much longer

and Sylvie Mercer who spent
her widow's pension on gifts
for the neighbours a steady stream
of Avon and Pot of Gold chocolates
like a Kwakiutl or Doukhobor
protesting no earth-licking fondness
for possessions going even one better
than Jesus by giving away her only coat

and I grew up reading *True Romance*
left in the bathroom by Carrie
who spun romance out of movies
and magazines from Tom's Store
while baking bread and jam jams
and pushing wet laundry through
the finger-crushing wringer
and listening to the stories of her
neighbours like a radio hotline host
and serving french fries to sons
who thought her kitchen was a take-out

and I grew up waiting for Skipper
who always woke early with dark
still filling the windows
and walked alone to the mill
through the warm hot cool cold seasons
and all day inhaled the heat and noise
of the world's biggest paper mill
his laughter still heard
over the endless pulse of machines
and at day's end burst into the kitchen
chased by the dark his face a grin

and I grew up with Carrie and Skipper
at the center of Mercer madness
listening to Sal while Billy
watched television and visiting
Dougie and Lil in the hospital
and sitting on the verandah
with Sam and delivering
Sylvie's gifts to the neighbours
and often I asked Carrie and Skipper
why do you put up with them
their only reply they're family
and on television I saw Neil Armstrong
walk on the moon and I know it is true
even though Billy Mercer still claims
it was all a hoax

FATHERS AND SONS

I dance with my son
afloat on whorls of music
like spun sugar,
his legs knotted around my waist,
his breath a blue fire on my neck:
perhaps we could dance
without end on a screw
in a box for keepsakes

but in my eye's rear-view
mirror, long ago,
I see my father sleeping
under his newspaper rising
and falling on gentle snores,
while I slip into his room
and with a carpenter's precise swing
wake him with a hammer blow

    at the time
    it too seemed
    a good idea

I STILL HEAR THE BELL RINGING

On long walks from Crescent Pond
in cool/warm Mays on the keen edge
of promised summer (our creels
heavy with a dozen trout more
than the law permitted) my father
offered the only advice I remember:

Take your garbage home,
and in my knapsack, then and now,
empty Vienna sausage cans,
wax paper, pop bottles

If you don't know a word,
look it up in a dictionary,
strong advice, for now I know
many words and in words I am known

Never hate anybody,
wisdom like an iron bell ringing
from a gray sky, its echoes
heard through the years

Never hate anybody
Never hate anybody
My one wish (who needs three?):
on long walks from Crescent Pond
through the dense spruce, across the bog
on a trail only my father could see,
I wish he had taught me how

NAN'S NOTE

1

I'm marching through the high grass
in Uncle Sam's yard on my way to Ro Carter's store
and I can't read my grandmother's note
because I know Nan is watching
from her window, is always watching,
and I need to read the note
(how else can I know if Nan is ordering
Fudgicles and macaroons and an apricot pie)
and hiking in the high grass, pretending
I'm David Livingstone hunting natives in need,
I can see the air, still gray
painted with the dust my father's Rambler
rumbled into the sky as it roared down Lynch's Lane,
my father's voice filling the air with scarlet words,
Carrie, if your mother turns up
the heat again, I'll saw the damn roof off,
my grandmother convinced that with the new hot air
furnace and a duct in every room she controls
the whole world with a plastic button on the wall,
and when cold turns the thermostat with a deft twist
like a Las Vegas shark at a roulette wheel
while my father groans, it's cooler
in the mill behind the pulp grinders
where, my father insists, men sometimes melt
and all that gets sent home is a shoe box
of teeth and finger-nails and toe-nails.

2

Ro Carter unfolds the note slowly
like a love letter he doesn't want,
closes one eye and rubs his tongue
around his teeth. Can't hardly
read your grandmother's writing.
A trap for a caribou?
No such thing, is there?
The note has one line:

(not Fudgicles and macaroons and an apricot pie)
 an ashtray with a caribou.
Well, I'll be darned,
the ashtray with the caribou.
Yes, yes, I've got it
poked away somewhere.
Years ago I got that ashtray.
For tourists. Couldn't sell it.
Didn't get any tourists.
Only Jehoshaphat knows where it is now.
Ro Carter closes the other eye
and stamps his feet.
Here it is. Right where I left it.
Your grandmother taking up smoking,
is she? I'll put it on her bill.

3

Pushing through the high grass in Uncle Sam's yard
I bear the ashtray wrapped in brown paper
and David Livingstone is no longer hunting natives
in need and the air is no longer gray and scarlet
with dust and words, my father faraway
in Birchy Cove sitting under a chestnut tree
with Uncle Jim and Fox and Bud who laugh a lot
and never touch thermostats, my father says,
and my grandmother smiles
when I give her the ashtray,
a bronze glass bowl with a leaden caribou standing
on the edge and grooves in the antlers to stick
burning cigarettes and a picture
of Bowater's Pulp and Paper Mill inscribing
a message in the air with ribbons of smoke:
Welcome to Corner Brook, but I don't ask Nan
about the Fudgicles and macaroons and apricot pie.

4

With the sun sinking
behind Blow-Me-Down Mountains
my father's Rambler slips up the lane
and my father slides into the living room,
adjusts the thermostat,
opens windows, grins at me.
This for me? From your grandmother?
He slips the string off the parcel,
all his actions slow and easy
like an Anglican pastor.
My father taps gently
on my grandmother's door,
looks in, Nan propped
up on four pillows
almost sitting in bed,
her head turned
toward the window,
eyes closed and breathing
with the rhythm of pretending
to be asleep.
Thanks, Missus, it's a lovely ashtray.
My father closes the door quietly.
I ask my father why Nan gave him
an ashtray even though he stopped
smoking two years ago.
His brown eyes are burnished
bronze like the ashtray.
Perhaps I'll take it up again, he says,
and perhaps tomorrow I'll charge
through the high grass in Uncle Sam's yard
with another note from my grandmother
for Fudgicles and macaroons and an apricot pie.

WHO'S AFRAID OF JACQUES COUSTEAU?

In the low summer sun my children
are walking a yellow road across the cove
plunging into the water away from me
sitting on the gray beach writing
a poem about long Sunday afternoons
in July and August when my father drove
my brother and me out of the city
through Gillams
     and Summerside
         to Wild Cove
so he could sit on the beach
and whittle boats out of driftwood
with jagged circles of tin for rudders
rigged with cereal box sails
  (Bobby Orr with strong knees
  laughing over a bowl of Wheaties)
launched without champagne
three or four at a time, all the same
while my brother and I swam
like Johnny Weissmuller and wrestled
crocodiles and buried one another
like the Cherokee buried their enemies
with just heads sticking out of the sand
so ants could eat their brains
  (my brother claimed ants would die
  from malnutrition in my head)
and my father baked in the sun
and whittled an armada of sailing ships
and for years Jacques Cousteau
shoving the Calypso through garbage
in the oceans of the world
has been cursing my father's boats
and now I write, the flotsam
of memories whittled and shaped
in words and set afloat.
  What will Jacques Cousteau
  say about my poems?

TANGLED

(Lines from Edmonton to my father in Newfoundland)

far away
in a city you will never know
I chase words in the cold air
  and measure my worth
  by the words made mine
  and remember you
    silent
crouched in the bow of a dory
rising and falling on blue-gray waves
in the air yellow-orange with the sun
untangling the line I twisted in knots
in my frenzy to tear from the ocean
a cod with a lead jigger hooked in its side
  and I remember you
    sat
and traced the line through its knots
and said nothing
and untangled my line
that could reach to the bottom of the ocean
and lay in swirls at your feet
untangled it
  in the morning sun
    through the noon sun
      into the afternoon sun
and said nothing
and I wouldn't look at you
because I knew you were mad
and I had to look
and you weren't mad
  you were smiling
and where I live now
there is no ocean
unless you stand on your head
and pretend the sky is ocean
  but it's not

and the line I throw out
never hooks into the sky
but always falls back
and tangles at my feet
and perhaps that's why
you could spend hours untangling
my tangled line
   you knew
an untangled line could be thrown
into the ocean's black silence
   and
anchor you to the bottom